IMPROVING MIDDLE SCHOOL INSTRUCTION:

A Research-Based Self-Assessment System

Judy Reinhartz
Don M. Beach

nea PROFESSIONAL LIBRARY
National Education Association
Washington, D.C.

The Advisory Panel

Johnny Blevins, Language Arts Teacher, Burnside School, Somerset, Kentucky

Dave L. Edyburn, Learning Disabilities Teacher, Rock Falls Junior High School, Rock Falls, Illinois

Stephen J. Taffee, Associate Professor of Education, North Dakota State University, Fargo

Barbara Zynda, Reading Consultant, MacDonald Middle School, East Lansing, Michigan

Copyright © 1983

National Education Association of the United States

Stock No. 1688-2-00

Note

The opinions expressed in this publication should not be construed as representing the policy or position of the National Education Association. Materials published as part of the Analysis and Action Series are intended to be discussion documents for teachers who are concerned with specialized interests of the profession.

Library of Congress Cataloging in Publication Data

Reinhartz, Judy.
   Improving middle school instruction.

(Analysis and action series)
Bibliography: p.
   1. Middle schools. 2. Teaching—Evaluation.
I. Beach, Don M. II. Title. III. Series.
LB1623.R44   1983   373.2′36   83–13364
ISBN 0–8106–1688–2

CONTENTS

PREFACE

The material for this manuscript was developed from two presentations made by the authors at the meetings of the Association for Supervision and Curriculum Development in Anaheim, California, in March 1982 and of the National Middle School Association in Kansas City, Kansas, in November 1982. The feedback from participants in each workshop session was especially helpful in developing the final manuscript.

After more than 30 combined years in the field of education, working with middle school teachers as colleagues, supervising teachers, and peers, we are convinced that teachers do indeed make a difference in student learning. Because of that belief, we are hopeful that the Self-Assessment System described here will be beneficial to all teachers as they work to help students learn.

The Authors

Judy Reinhartz is Associate Professor and Assistant Director for Field Experiences, Center for Professional Teacher Education, at the University of Texas at Arlington.

Don M. Beach is Dean of the School of Education at Tarleton State University, Stephenville, Texas.

THE MIDDLE SCHOOL:
THE TEACHING ENVIRONMENT

The school environment is an important aspect of the instructional process in the middle school. As a first step, then, it is necessary to examine the characteristics of the middle school before describing the procedures that teachers can use to improve their instruction.

The concept of the middle school is a rather recent development in American education. Throughout this century there has been a movement toward a third level of schooling, rather than two organizational patterns— grades 1 through 8 and high school. As the third level has evolved, it has usually been called the junior high school.

By the 1960s, however, the junior high arrangement of seventh, eighth, and sometimes ninth grades was under scrutiny. Many educators, dissatisfied with this grouping, felt that its content and methods were more suitable for high school students and that it failed to serve as a bridge between childhood and adolescence (46).* The criticisms often voiced about the junior high school program included the following:

- The rigid, departmentalized programs were more suitable for the intellectual development and social maturity of the high school student rather than the 9- to 13-year-old.
- Course content was a watered down version of high school studies and not appropriate for the preadolescent.
- An excessive emphasis on competition, particularly interscholastic sports, involved only a small percentage of students.
- Students were often divided or counseled into two different tracks, vocational and academic, very early in their schooling.
- A heavy emphasis on testing, grading, and group norms characterized the evaluation process.
- There was a lack of discussion about social behavior and peer interaction at a time when such discussions are essential to preadolescent development (60).

---

* Numbers in parentheses appearing in the text refer to the Bibliography beginning on page 60.

5

As a result of these and other criticisms, teachers and administrators began to recognize the need for an arrangement that would meet the special requirements of the preadolescent, the student ranging from 9 or 10 to 13 years of age. This recognition led to the reorganization of the junior high school and the emergence of the middle school, which was designed to provide curriculum and methods more suited to the developmental levels of the preadolescent.

Today, the middle school typically begins with grades 5 or 6 and continues through grade 8. This arrangement accommodates students with similar developmental needs and abilities. In 1977 15 states had 100 or more middle schools in operation, and several states reported over 200 (1). This grouping of grade levels has become even more widely accepted, so that today, 5,000 such organizational patterns are reported (46). The number of separate middle schools includes: grades 5 through 8, 1,024; grades 6 through 8, 3,070; grades 7 through 8, 3,070; grades 7 through 9, 4,004 (46).

Such recent growth makes it important to ask: How, then, does the middle school differ from the traditional junior high school in philosophy, curriculum, and instruction? What makes the middle school a unique environment for both teacher and student? According to Sale (60), an effective middle school should have the following ten major characteristics:

1. Programs and practices custom-designed and attuned to the growth and developmental characteristics of the preadolescent, with emphasis on the learner.
2. A curriculum that is intellectually stimulating, that has a variety of options and exploratory experiences, and that builds upon elementary learning rather than imitating the high school course of studies.
3. A school organizational pattern that incorporates both the security of self-contained classrooms as well as the benefits of interaction with a variety of teachers.
4. Health and physical education programs that emphasize physical fitness, personal hygiene, and lifetime sports as opposed to the competitive team sports of the high school.
5. Curricular experiences for all students that involve career exploration and interrelate academic areas with career options.
6. Teachers, administrators, guidance staff, and related school personnel specifically trained to work with preadolescents and cognizant of their developmental characteristics and needs.

6

7. Assistance to students in developing a good self-concept and in assessing social behavior and interaction with peers.
8. An evaluation program that places primary emphasis on student progress in relation to their own ability and secondary emphasis on assessment in terms of group norms.
9. Buildings and material resources adaptable to the needs of the preadolescent.
10. School and community programs that provide for successful citizen involvement in and support of school activities.

In addition, the middle school must also develop an instructional delivery system based on a variety of strategies that are appropriate for the preadolescent. Teachers must shed the common methods often used in the junior high school: lecture, listen, and take notes, or read the chapter and answer the questions.

Given the rapid growth of the middle school and its unique philosophical, curricular, and instructional characteristics, the problem confronting school districts has often been one of staffing the program with personnel who are trained for and committed to working with preadolescents. The typical dilemma has been whether or not to move an elementary teacher "up" or a high school teacher "down." In some situations, districts have established a middle school program, staffing it with teachers who have worked within the guidelines and framework of a junior high school model. The result has often been unsatisfactory for both students and teachers. According to Alexander and George (1):

> Many, probably most, of the personnel working in some 5,000 middle schools of today, did not originally choose to work at that level. They have learned almost all they know about middle school education through limited in-service education, and their experience. . . . (p. 20)

Part of the staffing problem stems from a lack of specific training for middle school teachers within professional preparation programs. The few junior high training programs have not been popular, and teacher certification agencies have been slow in introducing new programs for middle school certification (46). In a survey conducted by the National Association of Secondary School Principals in 1981, 41 percent of the principals reported that their teachers had no specific training for the middle school. Of those reporting some preparation, 72 percent indicated it was in-service training and only 44 percent included university courses (65). Undoubtedly most middle school teachers have been prepared for either elementary or high

7

school and their training for the middle school level has consisted of only brief in-service institutes or workshops.

Whatever their preparation, middle school teachers want and deserve sensible, practical advice about instructing preadolescents. The concerns of beginning teachers at this level can usually be summed up in one word—"Help." What advice should be offered? It often ranges from "Hang in there" to a step-by-step training program. The authors believe that this monograph fits somewhere between these two extremes. Throughout this text the message is that the teacher is in charge of the instructional process and is the key to the success of the middle school. Therefore, by having a knowledge of the history and expectations of the middle school movement and an understanding of the school environment, teachers can improve instruction in the middle school.

THE MIDDLE SCHOOL STUDENT:
TURNABOUT OR PREADOLESCENT?

Improving delivery of instruction in the middle school begins with an understanding of the student population. An effective middle school staff is therefore knowledgeable about the developmental stages of the preadolescent—cognitive, moral, and physical. It is also important to recognize typical behaviors and special needs.

Since preadolescents are changeable, with a seemingly boundless energy source, middle school organizational patterns and teaching styles should be geared to a wide range of developmental levels and needs. The instructional program should meet the unique maturational characteristics, varied learning styles and rates and backgrounds of this student population. The learner and life-learning experiences should be given top priority, along with a variety of learning options and resources available to staff and students. All the building designs and program planning are for naught unless the needs and interests of students become the focus of course organization and lesson planning.

The successful middle school also provides the context or framework in which students can develop meaningful relationships with peers and adults, as well as opportunities for making decisions. In addition, it provides students with the opportunity to develop a value system and an appreciation of the learning process—learning how to learn not only about the world, but also about the self.

During the middle school years major developmental changes occur. According to Forisha-Kovach (29), human development is

> . . . a series of qualitative changes in behavior which occur at different periods of life . . . If development were quantitative instead of qualitative, for example, [a pre]adolescent would simply know more. . . . Yet, because development is qualitative, [a pre]adolescent not only knows more, but also thinks differently about what is known (p. 22).

Middle school teachers, perhaps more than any others, therefore need to become aware of the unique developmental changes associated with the preadolescent. Such awareness will have an important effect on their behavior in the classroom, thus contributing to a successful instructional program.

9

COGNITIVE DEVELOPMENT

There are several theories of cognitive development with implications for those who work with preadolescents. Piaget described four stages in the development of the intellect: sensorimotor (0 to 2 years), preoperational (2 to 7 years), concrete operations (7 to 11 years), and formal operations (11 years and above). Since these stages are ranges or approximations, the concrete operations and the formal operations stages are of particular significance to middle school teachers because they overlap during the middle school years (21).

In the concrete operations stage, students are aware of alternative solutions to problems; they have the capacity to relate an event or thought to a total system of interrelated parts and to conceive of an event from beginning to end. In the formal operations stage students enter the world of ideas and concept formation; they take a systematic approach to problems and make logical deductions by implication. Logical deductions help them understand the physical and social world and to acquire many new values (60). Deduction by hypotheses and judgment by implication enable them to reason beyond cause and effect.

Middle school teachers can implement Piaget's ideas by asking students to describe situations and events rather than to explain them. Propositional thinking and detailed explanations are possible only during the formal operations stage and the preadolescent may be in a period of transition (21).

Another important difference during the middle school years is students' use of language. Teachers can easily be misled by the verbal facility of their students, especially if they do not question them closely. During this transition period youngsters may use a term correctly with varying degrees of comprehension (21). The Piagetian-style classroom places less emphasis on the transmission of knowledge through the lecture-discussion method and more on the teacher's serving as a catalyst in situations where students become actively involved in their own learning (21).

Finally, Piaget's delineation of the stages of conceptual development and the complexity of subject matter imply that middle school teachers should be knowledgeable about what and how they teach. According to this view, the ideal learning situation arises from a match between the subject matter and the students' level of conceptual development:

A teacher who uses the best textbooks available and develops the most interesting and stimulating lesson plans can still fail to reach a majority of students in his class who do not have the necessary structures (operations) to enable them to "understand" the presented material. (21, p. 321).

Thus, it is important that teachers assess students' developmental level and plan accordingly. Because of the wide range of differences in preadolescents, it may be necessary to plan and develop a wide range of classroom learning activities.

Havighurst has advocated the developmental task theory of growth: "A developmental task is a significant accomplishment that an individual must achieve by a certain time if he is going to meet the demands placed upon him by society" (60, p. 29). One of the major developmental tasks of preadolescence is the organization of the individual's knowledge of social and physical reality. During the transition from childhood to adolescence, students develop an interest in ordering, organizing, and systematizing knowledge. They become increasingly selective in what they will study. One student may like science; another, local history; another, team sports. All may want to explore subjects in greater depth and may seek a classification system for new knowledge.

In applying Havighurst's theory to the middle school, it is important that teachers provide a rich environment for exploration. Preadolescents need the opportunity to explore topics of interest by pursuing projects of their own choosing. They need situations where they can function in groups as they attempt to define social realities and to experiment with social roles and relationships. Middle school can serve as the ideal environment for exploring a variety of roles, including leadership, within the classroom structure. Students can be aides or laboratory assistants, or whatever gives them status and role identification in a class. As teachers present content, it is also important to provide the conceptual or organizational framework. Because most class time is often spent on learning specific terms or dates, preadolescents sometimes fail to see the organizational pattern or the whole picture of what they are studying.

A third developmental theorist, Bruner (14), suggests the possibility of teaching meaningful aspects of a subject at any age and at any developmental level if the presentation mode is suitable for the level. He identified three basic developmental modes for learning: enactive, knowing something through doing it; iconic, knowing something through a picture or image; and symbolic, knowing something through symbols such as language (15).

Thus, one might learn the concept of swimming through doing it

11

(enactive); through viewing a filmstrip on swimming techniques (iconic); or through reading a book on the topic (symbolic). . . . Enactive representation is dominant during infancy and early childhood; iconic representation becomes the norm through preadolescence; thereafter, symbolic representation dominates. (49, p. 205)

Bruner's view suggests an emphasis on visual learning in middle school. If preadolescents learn primarily through the iconic mode (through pictures), then classrooms should contain many illustrations of the concepts and principles being studied.

Utilizing Bruner's concept of the spiral curriculum, the notion that "any subject can be taught effectively in some intellectually honest form to any child at any stage of development," the middle school should structure course offerings that build upon principles and concepts students will continually encounter. Once students have learned something at a simplified level in the elementary school, they should be able to return to the topic at a more advanced level in middle school. In other words, they need to study the basic principles of a discipline over and over at different grade levels, but at higher levels of complexity and in greater depth (21). This spiraling effect can be particularly useful for teachers developing curriculum units that provide more in-depth study of recurring topics.

Erickson (26, 27), a fourth developmental theorist, has identified eight stages of human development from infancy to old age: (1) trust versus mistrust (infancy), (2) autonomy versus shame and doubt (first year of childhood), (3) initiative versus guilt (early childhood), (4) industry versus inferiority (school age to puberty), (5) identity versus role confusion (adolescence), (6) intimacy versus isolation (early adulthood), (7) generactivity versus stagnation (mature adulthood), and (8) integrity versus despair (older adulthood).

An understanding of Erickson's fourth and fifth stages can be helpful to the middle school teacher. In the fourth stage, industry versus inferiority, the skills necessary for life and family are developed. Young people (preadolescents) seek to integrate their past experiences and future expectations into a new sense of self. A "self" is shaped by the expectations of society and involves not only past and future, but also society (29). Because of the unique program of the middle school, teachers can be instrumental in helping students understand themselves—in terms of what they have been and what they might become. The fifth stage, identity versus role confusion, incorporates the building blocks for later resolution of issues confronting the individual such as clarification of sex roles, feelings of acceptance or rejection by the peer group, development of personal competency, obtaining success and achievement, understanding of bodily changes, and identification with an adult model.

Finally, the recent research on brain growth cautions middle school educators not to challenge learners at an unachieveable level of difficulty. Epstein (24, 25) suggests that the human brain grows in spurts rather than in simple linear increments across time. These brain growth spurts can be compared with Piaget's stages of cognitive development (12). Toepfer (64) summarizes the dichotomy between brain growth and school practices, stating that the problem within the middle school is due to the nature of educational programming offered during the 12 to 14-year age group span. Achievement and growth during the 10 to 12-year age group seems to confirm that emerging adolescents have the capacity to learn new and higher-level thinking skills along with acts and information. But the fact that they reach a brain growth plateau during the 12 to 14-year period indicates that they cannot continue to grow and develop new and higher-level cognitive and thinking skills as they did during the brain growth period of ages 10 to 12.

While the danger of overchallenging students during the brain growth plateau period is real, the application of the new data to the middle school does not mean that formal intellectual operations should be eliminated. Middle school teachers should be concerned with developing a broad curriculum that allows for personal student involvement. Such a curriculum is necessary because added years of exposure to the world through television, movies, reading, and relationships with adults have given middle school students greater stores of information and an increased natural curiosity (1). As they plan instruction, then, it is important that teachers recognize their students' variations in previous experience, knowledge, and potential for higher-level thinking and problem solving, and provide appropriate learning opportunities to foster their cognitive development.

MORAL DEVELOPMENT

Kohlberg (41) presents a theory of moral development based on the belief that morality is a set of rational principles for making judgments about behavior. He developed his theory by presenting moral dilemmas to children at different age levels. (21, p. 34). According to Kohlberg, moral development occurs in a series of six stages as students refine their concept of justice:

Stage 1. A punishment and obedience orientation in which one responds to a moral conflict in terms of a superior power, possible physical consequences of an action, especially the avoidance of punishment.

Stage 2. An egoist, relativistic orientation in which the guiding principle is "you scratch my back and I'll scratch yours."

Stage 3. The "good boy-nice girl" orientation in which action springs from a need for the approval of others.

Stage 4. A "law and order" stance in which right behavior consists of doing one's duty toward authority, rules, maintaining social order.

Stage 5. The social-contract, legalistic orientation in which right action is defined in terms of maintaining the social order and guaranteeing individual rights on the basis of using legal channels and socially agreed upon vehicles in changing a law, for example.

Stage 6. Here, the right is defined in terms of self-adopted ethical principles, especially the principle of justice, which respects the dignity of the individual as well as going beyond personal needs or whims and the opinions of others. (10)

By asking students about moral issues and listening to their responses, middle school teachers can gain insight into their level of moral thought. The procedure of posing moral dilemmas as suggested by Kohlberg can provide a basis for classroom discussions on such issues as capital punishment, abortion, death and the right to die, surrogate motherhood, genetic engineering, and drug usage. The purpose of such discussions is not to provide "right and wrong" answers per se but to raise the individual's level of moral reasoning (44). Kohlberg also urges teachers not to overemphasize classroom rules and routines because they may apply only to school situations; rather, he suggests allowing students to deal with situations posing broad problems and issues (21).

PHYSICAL DEVELOPMENT

The physical development and characteristic behavior of the preadolescent have been summarized by Jenkins, Schacter, and Bauer (35). The preadolescent period begins sometime between the ages of 9 and 13 with boys generally entering this stage two years later than girls. A middle school student may begin this period with the body "at rest." Although there may be no significant gain in weight or height, subtle changes are occurring in the physique. Then a period of rapid growth in height and weight follows, during which time girls are usually taller and heavier than boys. The reproductive organs start to mature and secondary sex characteristics begin to develop (pubic hair, menstrual cycle, voice change, facial hair). Students have unpredictable appetites; one minute they will eat anything and everything, the next, they will not touch a bite. Other physical characteristics include rapid muscular growth and uneven growth of body parts.

There is perhaps greater diversity in individual differences during this stage of development than at any other. Not only are there physical differences between boys and girls, but within each group are wide ranges of differences—physical, emotional, intellectual, and social. Gangs continue to exist, although group loyalty is stronger in boys than in girls. Teasing and playful antagonism between boys' and girls' groups are common. Preadolescent behavior is characterized by awkwardness, restlessness, self-consciousness, and laziness which are common by-products of the physiological changes and rapid growth. Other characteristic preadolescent behavior includes interest in team games, pets, television, radio, movies, electronic games, and comics. Youngsters begin to value the opinion of the gang or peer group more highly than that of adults, and they are often overcritical, changeable, rebellious, and uncooperative.

Because of their unique physical development and behavior, preadolescent students have special needs that include a basic understanding by adults—especially by middle school teachers—of the physical and emotional changes. They particularly need warm, affectionate teachers with a sense of humor who do not nag, condemn, or talk down to them. They also need opportunities for greater independence and for assuming greater responsibility without excessive pressure. Finally, preadolescents need a sense of belonging and acceptance by peers.

The first, and perhaps most important, question for the middle school teacher to ask before going on is, "Do I like preadolescents?" The response is crucial because it affects interaction with students. The following questions have been provided to help teachers assess their understanding of middle school students.

How Well Do I Know My Students?

1. Do I understand the physical and emotional changes that occur in the preadolescent?
2. Do I provide opportunities within my classroom for independence and responsibility for each student?
3. Do I show warmth and humor as I work with students?
4. Do I refrain from nagging, condemning, or talking down to students?

5. Do I provide opportunities for students to feel a sense of belonging to the class or peer group?
6. Do I provide a wide range of learning opportunities to accommodate the wide range of individual differences?
7. Do I help students overcome self-consciousness about physical changes, awkwardness, and restlessness?
8. Do I help my students deal effectively with peer pressure?
9. Do I encourage students through my actions and assignments to be lifelong learners?
10. Do I provide opportunities for students to make decisions based on a value system?

THE MIDDLE SCHOOL TEACHER:
RESEARCH VARIABLES
AFFECTING TEACHING

As teachers begin the process of improving instruction, knowledge of the cumulative research data available can be very helpful to them. Research on instructional effectiveness is not new, but generic research that has been applied to the middle school is new. Research variables affecting teaching have their roots in educational supervision, observation, instrument development, and teacher evaluation (6).

The accumulated literature identifies a variety of ways for assessing the instructional performance of teachers. Various rating instruments have been used to evaluate generalized behaviors of effective teachers (16). Observation instruments have taken many forms, including the Flanders Interaction Analysis System (3) and the Observation Schedule and Record (OSCAR) (50). Other strategies for improving teacher effectiveness have included microteaching (2), clinical supervision (18), reflective teaching (19), and more recently, the Developmental Teacher Evaluation Kit (DETEK) (31). Each instrument seeks to collect and codify information about the teaching act to make decisions about teaching.

Although the models and strategies described are helpful in gathering data, the first step in developing a personal methodology for improving instruction is awareness of current research principles affecting teaching.

RESEARCH PRINCIPLES

While the development of the middle school organization is a recent phenomenon, the results of several decades of educational research are available to help teachers improve their classroom performance. Effective teaching behaviors are not based on myth and/or folklore; they have been derived from comprehensive reviews of research (48, 66, 55). This information can serve as a frame of reference.

Manatt (48) has listed 14 ascriptive teacher variables that correlate with effective teaching:

1. Superior knowledge of subject matter

2. High expectations of students
3. Using praise more than criticism
4. Spending less time on classroom management
5. Teaching to the class as a whole or to large groups
6. Using less seat work, but closely monitoring what is given
7. Selecting and directing activities, not students
8. Modeling what is to be taught
9. Using easy questions with a high success rate
10. Teaching until mastery of unit material is achieved
11. Using detailed lesson plans with a variety of activities
12. Spending part of each period preparing learners for learning
13. Providing ample opportunity to learn criterion material
14. Using responses that encourage students to elaborate upon answers.

In the selected summary of research cited by Walberg, Schiller, and Haertzel (66), 70 different teaching variables were analyzed. These authors listed the number of studies conducted for each variable and the percentage of studies that showed a positive effect on learning. The following list gives the teaching variables for which 90 percent or more of the studies indicated an impact on learning:

1. Time on learning
2. Curriculum innovation
3. Personalized systems of instruction (PSI)
4. Mastery learning
5. Revision of instruction based on achievement
6. Direct instruction on achievement
7. Lecture versus discussion on achievement
8. Student-centered versus instructor-centered discussion on attitude
9. Student-led versus instructor-led discussion on achievement and attitude
10. Factual questions versus conceptual questions on achievement
11. Effects of specific teaching traits on achievement—clarity, flexibility, enthusiasm, structuring
12. Psychological incentives—teacher's cues to students, teacher's engagement of class in lesson, each student engaged in lesson
13. Open education versus traditional education on creativity, attitude toward school, curiosity, independence, and cooperation
14. Motivation and learning.

From studies they reviewed, Rosenshine and Furst (55) identified nine variables associated with effective teaching:

1. Clarity of instruction
2. Explanation during instruction
3. Enthusiasm during instruction
4. Task orientation
5. Learning opportunities other than listening
6. Multiple levels of discourse
7. Use of student ideas
8. Use of noncritical remarks
9. Use of interesting questions.

The instructional behaviors of effective teachers come not only from research, but from classroom observation and statistical work. Most of the research yielding information about teaching and achievement gains are correlational studies which have been subjected to some criticism. The timeless argument about the relationship of cigarette smoking to lung cancer is an excellent example of a controversy which has not yet been resolved within the medical profession. In both cases—teaching behavior and learning gains, and cigarette smoking and respiratory health problems—correlational studies seem to produce consistent results. It is helpful to keep this analogy in mind when reviewing the following section.

CONSIDERATIONS FOR CONDUCTING A LESSON: A RESEARCH PERSPECTIVE

What was your favorite teacher like? What do you remember most about his/her teaching? Did you learn anything? The responses to these questions relate to the personal dimensions and outcome of teaching. The teacher you described may have had an instructional approach that helped you learn. The behaviors that you attributed to him/her should not differ significantly from those previously listed.

Effective teachers have been described as having a finite number of managerial, instructional, and organizational characteristics which differentiate them from ineffective teachers (53). Effectiveness is based on behavioral, situational, and trait theories of teaching (53). Effective teachers put students in touch with the curriculum and devise mechanisms to continue keeping them in touch.

Before teachers are ready to conduct a lesson, they need to identify student needs and abilities, especially those of middle schoolers, and plan what to teach. Many teachers believe that they know their subject and think well on their feet. For some, this may be true, but for others it is a delusion. Spontaneity and invention come only after planning. Plans become a script which can be used for improvising according to the situation. Only after understanding individual instructional techniques can teaching subtleties come forth. Along with the subtleties come confidence and effectiveness. In addition, detailed plans can be invaluable in saving teachers from embarrassment and humiliation.

Teachers have read articles, received handouts, and attended in-service sessions in which the message was clear—"Tips for Teachers." And their typical reaction has been "What else is new?" The answer to this is the emphasis on research related to effective teaching. The use of the recipe approach for tomorrow's class tends to reflect current educational trends. An understanding of this approach comes only with a knowledge of the research principles associated with the recipes, however. The principles are not new, but they tend to be consistent in producing positive results for teachers and students. They are "rules of thumb," not rules per se (23).

Theory guides teachers as they orchestrate the interaction of classroom life and activities. With skill, the movements create "an educationally productive tempo within a class" (23). Flexibility helps teachers adapt to unexpected opportunities. By using a variety of skilled behaviors, they can build up their "capacity to reach more students and to create a richer and more diverse environment for them" (38).

Within this context of a wide variety of teaching patterns, teachers should be aware of their own natural style and find ways to cultivate and enhance it. In the self-assessment system proposed, the ultimate goal of professional improvement is "to stimulate personal growth and nurture . . . [one's] unique potential" (38).

Where Do I Stand?

Directions: Read each statement and rate yourself according to the scale below.

5 = All the time	2 = Almost never
4 = Most of the time	1 = Never
3 = Sometimes	0 = Does not apply

___ 1. I plan detailed lessons based on the identified needs and abilities of my students.

___ 2. I rely on spontaneity when presenting a lesson.

___ 3. I am flexible when responding to students and when making provisions for learning options.

___ 4. I recognize the research principles related to effective teaching as guides for making instructional decisions.

___ 5. I read at least one article in a professional journal every month.

___ 6. I am eager to include a challenging situation or problem in my class.

___ 7. Based on my reading in professional journals, I incorporate something new (interesting story, new strategy, new information) in my plans.

___ 8. I attend nonrequired workshops, seminars, classes and/or conferences in my subject area.

___ 9. I feel that reading professional journal articles or books makes a difference in my teaching.

___10. I conduct research in my classes at least once in an academic school year.

By applying the information uncovered from over 200 research studies, middle school teachers can develop and practice generalized teaching behaviors to diagnose strengths and weaknesses. Nine process variables or principles identified by Rosenshine and Furst (55) have been selected because of their generalizability and recurrence in more recent studies. Process variables are teacher skills that are involved in the teaching-learning process and are positively correlated with student achievement. In the following pages, these variables are discussed, further developed, and specifically applied to improve middle school instruction.

Each variable also includes a list of descriptors which should be helpful to middle school teachers. By incorporating some of these behaviors into their existing repertoire of skills, teachers can form a productive eclectic base for deciding the appropriate types of teaching "moves."

PROCESS VARIABLES FOR IMPROVING MIDDLE SCHOOL INSTRUCTION

1. Clarity of Instruction

The first essential quality of effective teachers is a concern for long-term goals. Each day becomes the means for bringing students closer to these goals. Concerned teachers teach with one eye on the future, never losing sight of the goal of helping students become the best they can possibly become. In the overall scheme, then, day-to-day events must be executed with precision so that learning can take place. Students whose teachers lack clarity of instruction do not have a clear understanding of what is expected and do not know where they are going in terms of course content. It is the teacher's responsibility to make sure that students understand the course objectives as related to the sequence of events and the content to be learned, to provide the direction for moving toward a goal or goals.

Clarity of instruction is a necessary skill if students are to learn. The middle school teacher who is clear—

a. Reviews procedures, information, and/or directions before moving to new material.

b. Gives simple, concise directions and may list them on the chalkboard.

c. Rephrases questions, often repeats statements, and encourages students to ask questions.

d. Uses many examples to explain a point in a less abstract and confusing way.

e. Paces the lesson to coincide with varying rates of learning (39).

f. Establishes smooth transitions from subject to subject and situation to situation (4).

g. Expects students to learn and communicates this expectation.

h. Plans—including short- and long-term goals, behavioral performance objectives (66), a description of methods, content, and evaluation system.

22

i. Has organizational skills and attends to detail. Medley (51) found that effective teaching is more evident in a structured, well organized environment. "Good organization . . . is good instruction" (13).

j. Explains how the work is to be done.

2. Explanation During Instruction

Support for this variable can be found in research on encoding and decoding information. Teachers cannot assume that students understand what is being said because it may seem to be obvious. Therefore, when teachers teach too fast, something happens—students become confused and shut the teacher out and off. Teachers need to be sensitive to these behavior changes. They need to be prepared to say, "Wait a moment, I have lost them"—to "read" the qualitative cues within each situation (23).

The middle school teacher who is concerned about providing explanations to promote student learning—

a. Adjusts the instructional level to match the attention spans of students.

b. Follows an instruct-practice-instruct-reinforce procedure.

c. Modifies strategies to better communicate information.

d. Uses visuals, chalkboard, and several examples to provide a step-by-step approach when explaining information.

3. Enthusiasm During Instruction

Of the nine process variables, enthusiasm during instruction may be one of the most important. This assumption is supported by research studies uncovered by Ryans (59), Rosenshine (54), Rosenshine and Furst (55), and Medley (51). According to the studies on teacher effectiveness, enthusiasm seems to increase recall, produce comprehensive learning gains, improve attitudes, and increase divergent thinking. Walberg, Schiller, and Haertzel (66) found that enthusiasm positively affects learning; there is, in fact, a 100 percent correlation.

The enthusiastic middle school teacher—

a. Smiles a great deal and makes learning fun.

b. Is alert and full of energy, excited about what is being taught, exciting to listen to and watch.

c. Is motivated, motivates others, and shows interest in his/her subject.

d. Maintains eye contact.

e. Modulates voice level by volume and rate.

4. Task Orientation

Whether the term is task orientation, time on task, and/or academic learning time (17), we shall operationally define it as time during which students are actively and productively engaged in learning enterprises which can be traced to well-defined instructional objectives. During this time disruptions are greatly reduced and students are not idle and bored—for example, waiting for papers to be graded or waiting for further instructions from the teacher. It should be noted that in an average school year of 170 days, with 120 hours of mathematics (based on one 45-minute period each day), students are on task for a total of only about 37 hours (17).

This variable has significant implications for middle school teachers who want to become more effective in the classroom. Certainly if students are encouraged to devote their full attention to academic tasks, they should learn. Some educators suggest that more academic learning tasks would result in changes in achievement scores (17, 66).

Time on task may also include seatwork with the teacher regularly communicating with each student and monitoring individual progress. Within a businesslike, structured environment, there are choices, variety, and some flexibility. There is, however, no question that the teacher is the efficient manager of the instructional program, the materials, and the students. This does not mean that teachers shed their sense of humor at the classroom door. Laughing and joking are still pleasurable activities, in the right amounts and never at student expense. It is also important that teachers remember what it was like being a student.

The middle school teacher who places an emphasis on task orientation—

a. Plans activities that allow students to practice newly learned skills.
b. Monitors activities closely to ensure that students are completing the assignment.
c. Has students demonstrate skills to the class.
d. Regularly reviews assignments with students and incorporates activities in the evaluation system.
e. Conducts the classroom so that less time is spent on housekeeping chores such as taking attendance and distributing books and more time is spent on developing learning skills.

5. Learning Opportunities Other Than Listening

This process variable encourages teachers to develop a "pattern of teaching techniques" or clusters of behaviors (28). The patterns vary according to the subject, the learning task, the developmental levels and learning styles of the students, and philosophy of the local school district.

A common misconception held by many educators and often supported in professional journals is endorsing a "one-method-that-can't-miss" philosophy. Upon careful analysis, one method does not fit all, students or teacher. What works well with one group one day may not work with the same group the next week. Consequently teachers need a "pattern of teaching techniques," including small groups activities, creative dramatics, role playing, and the like. It is an indisputable fact that "procedures always affect outcomes" (34).

The continuum represented in Figure 1 graphically demonstrates what Joyce and Weil (38) call a "cafeteria of alternatives" for teachers. The range of methods is not exhaustive, but it serves to illustrate the broad base of alternatives that teachers can select from. With these alternatives, it is possible to view teaching in pluralistic terms. Oftentimes teachers strive for the "perfect" method, but they soon find that none can satisfy all types of learning. Growth in teaching requires that teachers become multifaceted learners; an awareness of such a continuum of teaching methods is a place to begin.

Small group activities such as panel discussions, laboratory experiments, and games give preadolescents an opportunity to expend energy, engage in decisionmaking, overcome shyness and be boisterous. Creative dramatics, choral reading, and role playing encourage them to express their feelings, likes, and dislikes in an acceptable manner, behind the mask of a character. With assistance in how to take notes, the lecture, using advance organizers, can be an effective technique to use with middle schoolers. Advance organizers are principles or generalizations which are at a level of abstraction higher than the learning task itself (38).

By varying the combination of memory and drill work with interpretation and synthesis, learning gains occur. Studies concerning the use of a disproportionate number of drill activities indicate that "more" is not necessarily better for producing learning gains (56). Moderation seems to be advisable.

It has been shown that teacher movement and interaction with students during seatwork—in reading, for example—result in higher gain scores. There seems to be no effective substitute for teachers' active in-

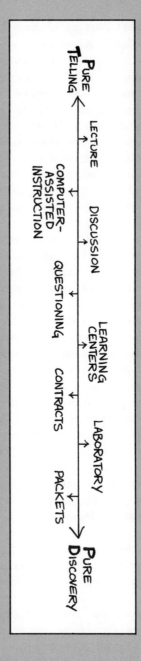

Figure 1
CONTINUUM OF TEACHING METHODS

26

volvement with students. Presence alone is not enough; teachers must act as catalysts if learning is to occur (51). In fact, at the middle school level there are negative indicators when teachers grade papers during class time (63). On the other hand, some consideration should also be given to independent work for preadolescents to pursue topics of interest with little, if any, teacher direction.

Homework or class assignments, particularly at the beginning of the school year, should be easy to complete and take a minimum of time. As the year progresses, the assignments should become gradually more complex.

Developing a pattern of teaching techniques enables teachers to become more flexible in their delivery of instruction as they make accommodations for the various learning modalities. As the old saying points out, "the best-laid plans" have a way of yielding to interruptions—picture taking, blaring announcements, pep rallies, and money-making projects. Contingency plans are therefore necessary and they do not come without some preparation. Teachers need to have several options ready to ensure that classes are interesting and worthwhile.

The middle school teacher who provides learning opportunities other than listening—

    a. Varies the pace of instruction in the classroom through lecture, practice, and group interaction.
    b. Considers student needs and incorporates student interests in lesson planning.
    c. Uses community resources in presenting subject matter.
    d. Provides opportunities for projects as a way to demonstrate knowledge.
    e. Develops a repertoire of teaching skills and activities.
    f. Provides for flexible and adaptable classroom arrangements.

6. Use of Multiple Levels of Discourse

This variable encourages teachers to appeal to all or several of the senses when delivering instruction. Presenting material so that students can see it, touch it, hear it, and/or smell it makes learning more lasting and fun. This is particularly important with preadolescents who may still be functioning at the concrete level of the cognitive domain.

Sometimes adults are temporarily fooled into believing that since preadolescents can act mature socially, they are intellectually more advanced. Concrete experiences followed by more abstract ones provide the

27

appropriate sequence for the occurrence of intellectual development. The objective is to help develop a process of thinking, not only of "right answers."

The middle school teacher who incorporates multiple levels of discourse in lessons—

a. Provides visual examples of the concepts being studied.

b. Has students simulate an event or a situation.

c. Provides demonstrations or laboratory situations.

d. Helps students analyze issues and discusses feelings and opinions.

e. Provides hypothetical situations and asks students to predict outcomes.

7. Use of Student Ideas

Using student ideas (8) is a positive statement to preadolescents that their opinions are respected and the teacher is willing to incorporate them into the instructional sequences. Middle school teachers who listen to their students model traits of patience and understanding. They communicate that students are important and have worth and dignity.

Patience is as important for middle school teachers as it is for kindergarten teachers. Students may not understand a concept the first time it is presented, for example. Such patience and understanding are different from being a student's "pal," however. The middle school teacher is in charge and never abdicates his/her position—this would result in an agonizing year for both teacher and students. The teacher's job is not to win a popularity contest, but to help preadolescents bridge the developmental isthmus from childhood to adulthood. In some cases, the teacher may be the only responsible adult model in the student's life.

Many teachers strongly believe in the use of student ideas, but have difficulty implementing this variable. Since there is always time pressure to cover a specific amount of content, teachers can compensate by using wait time, a three- to five-second pause between questions and responses during a lesson (57). The effects on both teacher and student behavior are phenomenal. The most important are as follows:

a. Teachers have more time to process comments and formulate higher-order questions.

b. Students have time to think about the topic and how they feel about it.

c. The level of confidence in students increases.

28

Finally, planning a time for discussions is a must, perhaps not everyday, but certainly sometime during the course of a week.

The middle school teacher who uses student ideas—
a. Regularly solicits suggestions or examples from students during class discussions.
b. Has students bring examples from home to supplement what is being studied and asks them to comment on each example.
c. Has groups of students plan activities for each unit of study.
d. Has students anonymously comment on or evaluate each unit.
e. Uses a suggestion box.

8. Use of Noncritical Remarks

This variable determines the emotional climate of a classroom and thus influences learning (62). When teachers harshly rebuke students for disruptive behavior, a negative learning climate results. Despite a lack of data for the notion that a positive learning climate increases student learning, there is sufficient data to support the inverse—a negative classroom climate decreases student learning (62).

Preadolescents believe in justice and fairness. Therefore, wise teachers avoid having "pets." All students are different, and it may be tempting to single out "good" students because they are polite, cooperative, and eager to please. Students at this age quickly sense injustices, however. When teachers handle student responses and questions positively and enforce class rules consistently, preadolescents are more likely to consider such treatment impartial and fair.

The middle school teacher who avoids using critical remarks—
a. Works to develop a vocabulary of praise words (i.e., "Good comment," "Interesting idea," "Nice suggestion," "Great job").
b. Tries to identify something positive about each student and cultivates that trait.
c. Remembers that praise motivates and encourages students to learn.
d. Provides rewards (verbal and other) in class routine.

9. Use of Interesting Questions

This variable may be somewhat misleading. For discussion purposes, it relates to asking a broad range of questions which lessens the threat of failure and invites all students to participate. Calling on a student before asking a question gets all students involved, not only those who know the answer (30). Kounin (43) stresses "withitness" during instruction. Teachers who use this technique are continuously aware of what is transpiring in the classroom and communicate their awareness to students.

Current research indicates that teachers ask more recall/information questions than any other type—60 percent (30a). They ask probing questions only 20 percent of the time. Probing questions are open-ended, often without a right or wrong answer; they invite students to explore information and to supply the appropriate concepts and principles. Such questions are important because they improve student responses and help them demonstrate their understanding (45, 67). As the instructional process shifts away from the teacher-dominated classroom to one designed by the teacher with student involvement, questioning strategies can become useful teaching techniques.

The middle school teacher who improves questioning skills—

a. Prepares a list of questions for each lesson.
b. Examines the list of questions to ensure multiple levels of thinking (i.e., application, analysis, and evaluation).
c. Asks students to summarize and draw their own conclusions.
d. Asks "What would happen if . . .?"
e. Asks students to describe situations and examples.
f. Has students develop their own lists of questions about the topic.

Taken together, these nine process variables provide prescriptive guidelines for middle school teachers. Many of the guidelines overlap but are not contradictory. Several studies show significant progress toward linking such teacher behaviors to student learning (13a, 47, 55, 66).

It is hoped that these process variables will help middle school teachers discover the most worthwhile patterns of behaviors. Professional self-improvement requires a passion for excellence, more than mere copying: "Great teaching demands not only hard effort and dedication, but also a profound belief in the importance of learning" (58, p. 49). In other words, hard work combined with a commitment and zeal for teaching translates into greater competency and effectiveness.

MIDDLE SCHOOL INSTRUCTION: A SYSTEMATIC APPROACH TO TEACHER SELF-ASSESSMENT

The middle school environment, the learners, and the teachers are integral parts of the teaching-learning process. Teachers, however, make the difference (13). To be effective, teachers must be able to analyze their own classroom behavior and determine which course(s) of action to take instructionally. This examination process is a form of evaluation.

Evaluation is an essential part of the teaching-learning process within the middle school organization. There are two reasons for evaluating teaching: (1) to make judgments or summative decisions about retaining or dismissing a teacher during the stated probationary period; (2) to make staff development or formative decisions to help teachers improve their instructional performance.

Manatt (47) has characterized the evaluation process as a cycle. Although in some situations it is conducted by an objective observer, an administrator or supervisor, it is our belief that the evaluation cycle begins with the teacher. Therefore, it is important that teachers have the necessary skills for examining all aspects of their delivery system in order to make appropriate decisions about instruction.

While several evaluation systems are available, we do not necessarily advocate a single system; nor do we suggest that ours is the best way. The Self-Assessment System advocated here is designed for middle school teachers. The emphasis is on staff development and instructional improvement.

The decision to solicit information about teaching initiates the process. Teacher self-assessment has been defined as "the process of self-examination in which the teacher utilizes a series of sequential feedback strategies for the purpose of instructional self-improvement" (6, p. 9). In addition,

> . . . the purposes of teacher self-assessment are to enable the teacher to become aware of personal classroom effectiveness, learn how to control classroom instructional behaviors [and] become self-directed in improvement activities. (6, p. 9)

31

Since the middle school is designed to work with a special age group of students with unique developmental needs and characteristics, self-assessment for middle school teachers should be somewhat different from other evaluation systems. The system described here is designed to help teachers become aware of their own strengths and weaknesses as related to classroom instruction. We suggest combining the unique qualities necessary for working with middle school students and the characteristics of effective teachers as one way to begin self-evaluation. See Figure 2.

The first step in the Self-Assessment System is to solicit information for self-diagnosis and self-awareness. During this process, middle school teachers must use carefully developed inventory tools. These tools could be used by any classroom teacher, but they are particularly helpful to teachers who are experiencing difficulty, either because of low student achievement scores, insufficient student involvement, and/or parental/peer comments. Inventory items must be tied to research variables and be specific enough to force teachers to make critical decisions regarding their instructional efficacy. The results generated from this first step give teachers a beginning data base for developing an instructional profile.

Examples of personal inventories and lesson assessment instruments appear in Appendix 1. They are designed to gather information about teacher attitudes and instructional behavior. The items included in the inventories relate to the nine process variables. Teachers are encouraged to develop similar assessment tools that more closely parallel the objectives of their own school district and middle school.

If the data collected on the inventories are inconsistent with instructional performance, there is a misconception concerning personal classroom effectiveness. In such cases, it is necessary to work toward reconciling the self-perception with more objective measures. For example, the teacher may perceive himself/herself as fair, student-oriented, and committed to the middle school philosophy, while students or other school personnel may perceive the teacher as inflexible, too content-oriented, and too demanding. For the Self-Assessment System to work successfully, the teacher must be prepared to objectively compare the responses from both sources. The goal of self-assessment is not necessarily to have responses match—those of the teacher with those of others—but it is important to recognize such different perceptions, if they exist, and try to do something about them.

The discrepancy may be due to an individual's unwillingness to admit that there is a problem and marking himself/herself high on an

32

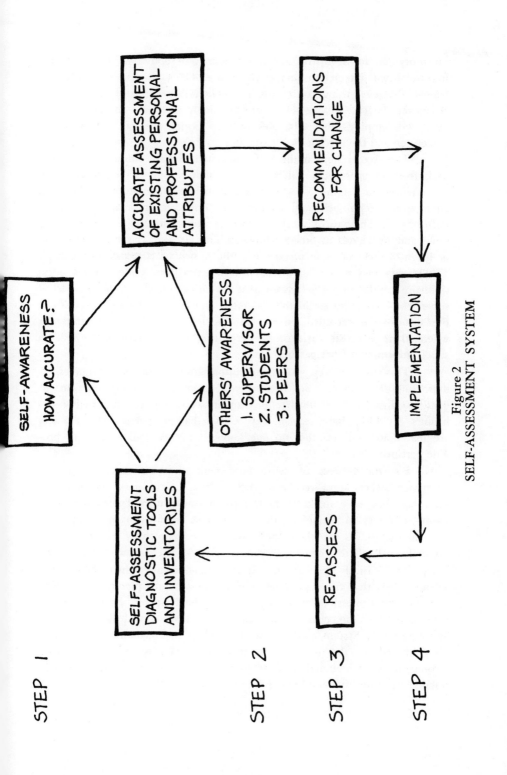

Figure 2
SELF-ASSESSMENT SYSTEM

inventory. Or during instruction a teacher may be oblivious to cues regarding classroom interaction and performance. Or a teacher may sincerely believe that everything concerning instruction is progressing satisfactorily. Whatever the case, teachers who are genuinely interested in self-improvement will employ other strategies to help bridge the gap between self-perception and the perceptions of significant others.

The second step in the Self-Assessment System thus involves feedback from other sources. Efforts such as videotaping or audiotaping can be beneficial in helping to develop a personal teaching profile. Video- and audiotaping techniques tend to be more objective in analyzing teacher performance. They also give the teacher an opportunity to see how he/she looks and/or sounds to others while teaching, as well as a chance to view or listen to these tapes in private with the option of later destroying them. The teacher may also wish to solicit comments from students on a questionnaire similar to the self-assessment inventory. Or she or he may ask a supervisor or peer to sit in the classroom and observe a lesson to validate the information recorded on the inventories. In unusual circumstances where there is great variance in perceptions, the teacher may wish to solicit information from parents.

This second step, collecting information from other sources, is most important in the Self-Assessment System. A common reaction, to guard against, is to rationalize or explain away ineffective teaching behaviors. At this point a teacher may believe that the perceptions of others are inaccurate and feel that no one knows him/her well enough to provide pertinent data.

For the process of self-improvement and self-assessment to be effective, teachers must recognize that it is a difficult task and must be sure that they have made an honest commitment toward changing classroom behaviors. Additionally, they must have confidence in the process and in themselves. If these two factors are objectively addressed, the original goal of the system—accurate self-assessment—can be achieved.

The critical moment in self-assessment comes when the teacher acknowledges that the system has yielded an accurate picture of existing personal and professional attributes. This is the time for the third step— formulating recommendations for change in instructional behavior. The Self-Assessment System comes to a close when the recommended changes are reflected in the teacher's instructional performance. Implementing recommendations and making changes in their instructional behavior help teachers learn to think and behave differently.

Instructional improvement relies on five components: "theory, demonstrations, practice, feedback and classroom application" (37). The magnitude of change may depend on the teacher's ability to accept feedback. With a structured and consistent feedback system, teachers can demonstrate and practice teaching skills in front of significant others—peers, supervisors, and/or professors. After this type of experience, teachers are more willing and likely to transfer skills they have practiced to the classroom. At first, however, until the rough edges are smoothed out, a new teaching technique or suggestion may feel awkward. A team of "coaches" can assist individual teachers in diagnosing small group demonstrations for content and variety of teaching strategies, for example. At this point the concept of "coaching" becomes a useful strategy for improving instruction, reconciling perceptions, and/or sharing mutual feelings and problems with other educators (36). Coaching provides a needed support system for teachers attempting to make changes in their instructional performance. Additionally, it adds an element of companionship which encourages teachers to share their successes and frustrations and to work out problems that may have surfaced during demonstration sessions. By adding the coaching element to the Self-Assessment System, teachers can seek assistance from experienced peers in an acceptable and nonthreatening manner. Sharing concerns and problems is a more pleasurable task than handling them alone. Team members also benefit by providing technical feedback.

The next section contains a case study that illustrates how middle school teachers can use the Self-Assessment System to improve classroom instruction.

THE SELF-ASSESSMENT SYSTEM: A CASE STUDY

The following description of a middle school teacher, Mr. Doe, elaborates on each step of the Self-Assessment System. It is an example of how the data collection process can be undertaken by middle school teachers to improve their classroom instruction.

As students enter the classroom, Mr. Doe usually greets them at the door, identifying each one by name. He begins each life science class with a lecture which includes a general overview of the concepts to be presented that day, listing on the chalkboard the major vocabulary words and concepts that will be encountered during the lesson. In each lesson, he stresses content. Mr. Doe plans activities that students can do during the lesson, particularly laboratory activities. He has a minimum of one lab activity a week, but usually at least two.

During the lesson, Mr. Doe stops periodically to ask if students have any questions before he moves on the next topic or concept. Students seldom respond to opportunities to elaborate on the material and rarely volunteer information or ask questions. When asked, they respond to direct questions. Mr. Doe communicates clearly to the class what he expects in the way of classroom conduct. He often discusses proper classroom conduct and consistently enforces class rules. The class atmosphere can be described as orderly and cooperative. Misbehavior is minimal.

As he begins a lesson, Mr. Doe usually stands behind the laboratory demonstration table. During his overview and lecture he seldom moves more than a few feet from the demonstration table to the chalkboard. Not only does he remain in the one area during the lesson, but his students also seldom move about the room. Students. move about only when laboratory activities are planned, at which time their movement is restricted to getting equipment and supplies.

Because of the nature of his subject, Mr. Doe feels that there is not enough student/teacher interaction. After his brief lecture, he would like his students to discuss the concepts presented. He is frustrated when they do not respond to his invitation to clarify the content when he asks, "Are there any questions?" He is not convinced that he has an adequate understanding of how well students know the information until he gives them a test. By that time, it is too late.

Student reluctance to participate in discussion, volunteer answers, or initiate questions is creating a problem for Mr. Doe. Consequently, he is beginning to question his effectiveness as a middle school teacher. While several students seem to do well in his classes, he concludes that most students could be doing much better. If he could get them to open up and talk about what they are studying, he thinks he would have a better indication of what they know. He is very concerned that his students do not appear to be motivated, are not responsive, and take a passive role in classroom activities. Mr. Doe would like his students to demonstrate some excitement about what they are studying.

Determined to do something about the situation, Mr. Doe decides to use the Self-Assessment System as a means of evaluating his teaching (see Figure 1 and forms in Appendix 1). The first step is to focus on the teacher, the self, to analyze or inventory current instructional practices, educational beliefs, and basic philosophies concerning the instructional process. (While the authors have included several forms to assess instructional performance in initiating the important first step of the Self-Assessment System, there are several commercially published inventories that teachers can use. Askins (5) suggests areas for self-assessment and lists appropriate instruments for collecting the data; information about these instruments along with their publishers appears in Appendix 2).

As Mr. Doe starts the first step of self-examination, he sits down in a quiet place and asks, "What am I doing instructionally?" The inventory "Diagnosing the Lesson," is particularly helpful here (see pp. 55–56). After careful reflection and frank answers to the questions on this inventory, Mr. Doe decides that he is rather low key when presenting material at the beginning of each class. Perhaps he is not showing any enthusiasm about the concepts to be studied. After all, some of the material is old hat to him; he has taught it four times a day for ten years. He is aware that he asks some specific content-related questions, but more frequently he asks, "Are there any questions?"

Next, Mr. Doe tries to determine how accurate his perceptions are about his teaching. One way to further validate the inventory is to tape a class or, better, several classes. The ideal situation would be to videotape a variety of his classes during the day. Videotaping can sometimes be disruptive or the equipment may not be available, however. A more modest, yet effective, way to tape the class is with a portable cassette tape recorder. Mr. Doe conceals a tape recorder in the classroom and records several lessons. Then he listens to the tape and analyzes the following areas:

1. How enthusiastic do I sound in introducing the lesson? Do I show excitement at what is to be studied for the day?
2. How many questions do I ask during the course of the overview and

37

lecture? How many are simple recall questions? How many are higher-order questions?

3. How do I respond to students when they answer a question? Do I encourage them in their responses? Do I wait for students to make a response? When students give a very good answer, do I tell them so?

4. What kinds of learning opportunities occur in the classroom? Are the majority of activities designed for students to sit and to listen?

5. Do I work with the class to summarize the lesson before making a homework assignment, class assignment, or move to another topic?

As he listens to the tape, Mr. Doe begins to compare his evaluation of the lesson with what he hears on the tape. This helps him decide, as best he can, what he is doing instructionally in the classroom that hinders student interaction and involvement in the lesson. If he is satisfied with the information and insights gained from the tape, he can proceed to Step 3, Developing Recommendations. If, however, he wants more information, he can initiate Step 2, Solicitation of the Perceptions of Others.

Mr. Doe rewrites the questions from "Diagnosing the Lesson" for students to complete. For example, the question "Was I enthusiastic in presenting the material?" he restates as "Was the teacher excited or enthusiastic while conducting the lesson?" Using this approach, Mr. Doe surveys his students and compares their perceptions with his.

Now he has two data bases to use to make judgments about his teaching effectiveness and his delivery of instruction. Other possible sources that contribute to the data collection process are colleagues and supervisors. Faculty members within the same school who teach the same subject are particularly helpful in providing information about Mr. Doe's instructional efficacy. Colleagues also provide support in deciding on ways to implement change in the lesson and can then help him assess the effectiveness of these changes. This coaching concept, discussed earlier, is a valid way to involve peers in the Self-Assessment System.

Now that Mr. Doe has collected his information and realizes that there are some things he can do to foster more student interaction, he moves to Step 3, Developing Recommendations. As he develops his list of recommendations, he tries to keep in mind that he does many instructional tasks effectively. He takes an interest in his students and conveys that interest as he greets them at the door. He carefully plans his instruction and makes every effort to have students learn about life science. He runs an orderly classroom relatively free from misbehavior and disruptions, which contributes to an effective learning environment. Clearly, Mr. Doe is not a poor teacher.

Nevertheless, he seems to be more concerned about teaching content than meeting the needs and interests of middle school students. As he develops his list of recommendations for improving his classroom instruction, he needs to be more aware of the developmental levels of his students, their physiological needs, and their intellectual development. He must be careful not to expect more from this age group than they are capable of delivering. Remembering that an effective teacher (a) asks a large number of questions, (b) probes for higher-order responses, and (c) provides for multiple levels of discourse, Mr. Doe develops the following recommendations:

1. When planning each lesson, Mr. Doe will write a large number of questions based on the lesson overview.
2. To complement the larger number of questions asked, Mr. Doe will formulate questions for each level of the cognitive domain to encourage higher-level thinking.
3. Mr. Doe will ask students to summarize the main points of the lesson before moving to another topic or activity. Remembering that pre-adolescents are better at describing rather than explaining, he will develop summary questions that have students describe rather than explain.
4. Periodically Mr. Doe will have students summarize the major points they have been studying by writing their answers on 5 x 8 cards. This will enable him to evaluate their knowledge and judge their level of mastery before giving them a test.
5. Mr. Doe will incorporate more visuals in his lessons; he will encourage greater student involvement by small-group work on assignments, work at the chalkboard, and content-related projects.

Now that Mr. Doe has completed the first three steps of the Self-Assessment System, he is ready to move to Step 4, the Implementation of the Recommendations. It is unrealistic to expect immediate success on every recommendation. In fact, it is sufficient to work on one or two recommendations at a time in order not to become discouraged about not bringing about change as rapidly as anticipated. After a reasonable period of time, perhaps several weeks, Mr. Doe can tape his classroom again to check on progress in his delivery of instruction and improvement in student involvement in the lesson. If there has been noticeable improvement, he has completed the four steps in the Self-Assessment System.

In summary, improving instruction in the middle school is a complex, yet challenging, task. The Self-Assessment System offers middle school teachers a positive, nonthreatening approach to self-improvement. Its undergirding philosophy is teacher self-awareness and an objective perception of the instructional self based on research principles. Competency in self-assessment comes with practice. It requires a willingness on the part of the teacher to engage in a step-by-step system on a regular basis in order that continuing instructional improvement and change may take place. As middle school teachers complete the Self-Assessment System, they become more aware of their particular teaching style. This aware-ness· can help them develop individual long-range plans that benefit their students, the middle school curriculum, and the middle school environment.

School districts, too, can benefit from developing long-term staff development programs that provide a supportive, nurturing environment in which to implement on a continuous basis these newly acquired and practiced teaching skills. Time invested in teacher self-improvement is time well spent on improving the overall quality of the instructional pro-gram in the middle school.

APPENDICES

1. SELF-ASSESSMENT SYSTEM INSTRUMENTS

SELF-ASSESSMENT INVENTORY

Name: _____ Date: _____

Circle your answers to the following questions to assess the components of your lesson. Use the following scale:

Always		Sometimes			Never
1	2	3		4	5

1. Did I perceive students as capable of accomplishing?   1   2   3   4   5

2. Was I open to student feedback?   1   2   3   4   5

3. Did I present content in appropriate ways to promote student understanding?   1   2   3   4   5

4. Did I follow up instruction with reasonable and interesting assignments?   1   2   3   4   5

5. Did I give individual help when students did not appear to understand?   1   2   3   4   5

6. Was I knowledgeable about concepts taught?   1   2   3   4   5

7. Did I regularly state expectations for classroom conduct?   1   2   3   4   5

8. Did I state expectations for content? Learning?   1   2   3   4   5

9. Did I monitor classroom behavior closely through movement and nonverbal behavior?   1   2   3   4   5

10. Did I accomplish objectives and complete instructional tasks?   1   2   3   4   5

11. Did I help students accomplish objectives and produce achievement in students?   1   2   3   4   5

12. Considering all above items, did I exemplify the characteristics of good teaching?   1   2   3   4   5

43

CLASSROOM LEADERSHIP INVENTORY

Complete the following inventory based on the way you conduct your classroom.

1. Are you sensitive to the feelings of your class as a group? YES NO

2. Do you listen to your students attentively? YES NO

3. Do you refrain from ridiculing members of the class? YES NO

4. Do you help each member of the class feel important and needed? YES NO

5. Do you refrain from arguing with the class? YES NO

6. Do you make sure that everyone understands not only what is needed, but why it is needed? YES NO

7. Do you recognize that everyone is important and needs recognition? YES NO

8. Do you share your classroom leadership by cultivating leadership in your students? YES NO

9. Do you develop long-range and short-range objectives for the class? YES NO

10. Do you share opportunities and responsibilities? YES NO

11. As you work to solve problems, do you break big problems into smaller ones? YES NO

12. Do you plan, act, followup, and evaluate? YES NO

PERFORMANCE CHECKLIST

This checklist might be helpful as you listen to an audiotape or view a videotape. Check the most appropriate column after reading each descriptor.

Needs improvement	Satisfactory	Outstanding	
			1. Provide an introduction to each lesson (establishing SET).
			2. Establish rapport with students to get them involved in the lesson (establishing SET).
			3. Relate present material to that previously learned (establishing APPROPRIATE FRAMES OF REFERENCE).
			4. Synthesize major points of the lesson by making cognitive links between past knowledge and new knowledge (achieving CLOSURE).
			5. Recognize and become sensitive to pupil behavior by noting visual cues such as boredom, bewilderment, facial expression (ATTENDING TO CLASSROOM BEHAVIOR).
			6. Encourage questions and respond to them (accepting STUDENT FEEDBACK).
			7. Reinforce desired student behavior (implementing REWARDS).
			8. Encourage students to join in discussions by offering comments and asking questions (establishing CLASSROOM INTERACTION).
			9. Use examples and illustrations to verify and/or substantiate concepts.
			10. Employ silence which encourages students to think or prepare responses and arguments (using WAIT TIME).

HOW DO I RATE?

Directions: Plot on the graph the number of times you use each of the following strategies in your classroom over the course of one week.

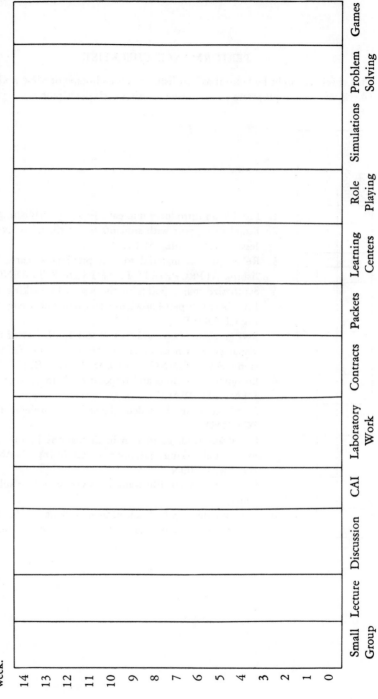

	Small Group	Lecture	Discussion	CAI	Laboratory Work	Contracts	Packets	Learning Centers	Role Playing	Simulations	Problem Solving	Games
14												
13												
12												
11												
10												
9												
8												
7												
6												
5												
4												
3												
2												
1												
0												

EFFECTIVE TEACHER INDICATOR SCALE

Name: _____   Date _____   Grade Level/Subject: _____

Directions: Decide which set of descriptors best describes your teaching behaviors.

Teaching Behaviors/ Characteristics	1	2	3	4	5
A. Giving directions and assignments	Unplanned.	Uses homework as a threat; is unclear.	Plans illustrations.	Provides clear examples.	Plans, illustrates, and motivates students.
B. Teacher movement	Avoids personal contact.	Restricted.	Not correlated with teaching purpose.	Moves freely and often.	Moves purposefully, enhancing interaction.
C. Verbal interaction	Talks most of the time.	Relies on volunteers.	Limited, calls on students.	Varied.	Encourages a variety of verbal interaction.
D. Instructional strategy	Relies on recall, texts, and worksheets.	Summarizes and puts into own words.	Has students compare and contrast.	Has students solve problems.	Promotes activities leading to decisionmaking and problem solving.
E. Empathy	Has little or no concern and makes little or no effort to understand student values.	Polite and concerned.	Shows concern, but makes no effort to understand.	Shows concern for individuals.	Shows concern about individuals and makes an effort to understand student values.
F. Tolerance	Discriminates.	Shows favoritism.	Ignores students.	Interacts with students.	Accepts all students.
G. Manner	Defensive and hostile.	Indifferent.	Businesslike.	Confident with sense of humor.	Relaxed, confident, displays sense of humor.
H. Classroom management	Chaotic.	Unfair in enforcing consequences.	Tolerates misbehavior.	Consistent in enforcing consequences.	Consistent and encourages self-direction.
I. Language	Ridicules and criticizes.	Enforces etiquette.	Offers alternatives.	Accepts content.	Accepts and extends content.
J. Reinforcement	Critical and/or sarcastic.	Gives a nonresponse (i.e, OK).	Accepts and encourages students.	Praises, encourages, and is humorous.	Accepts, encourages, and praises students.

RECORD OF LESSON CONTENT AND ORGANIZATION:
TOPICAL DATA COLLECTION

Name: _____ Date: _____

Lesson Topic: _____ Class Size: _____

Record student behavior and classroom interaction (classroom management data).

List information pertinent to concepts presented (knowledge of subject matter data).

Identify distracting actions and mannerisms (personal characteristics data).

Plot teacher movement (teacher mobility data).

TIME ON TASK: A TIME LINE

Name: _____ Date: _____

Lesson Topic: _____ Class Size: _____

Directions: Record the time of each transition, describe the transition, and the
nature of the task.

Time	Description of Transition	Nature of Task

COMMENTS:

CLARITY OF INSTRUCTION—TEACHER FORM

Name: _____ Date: _____

When trying to improve instruction, it is helpful to ask yourself the following questions.

Directions: Use the scale below to rate your level of Clarity during a lesson. Include written comments to help interpret the numerical rating.

5 = All the time	2 = Almost never
4 = Most of the time	1 = Never
3 = Sometimes	0 = Does not apply

	Rating	Comment
1. I have a detailed plan to follow.		
2. I explain the information simply and carefully.		
3. I use examples that students understand.		
4. I use a step-by-step procedure throughout the lesson.		
5. I encourage students to ask questions when they do not understand.		
6. I stay with a concept until students understand.		
7. I repeat terms, provide several examples, and use visuals when students do not understand.		
8. I stop often to review information before moving on to a new topic.		
9. I ask questions to determine the level of understanding.		
10. I stress the important points to remember.		

CLARITY OF INSTRUCTION—STUDENT FORM

I would like your assistance to improve the teaching skill Clarity of Instruction. Read the following statements and rate each one according to this scale:

5 = All the time	2 = Almost never
4 = Most of the time	1 = Never
3 = Sometimes	0 = Does not apply

IT IS EVIDENT DURING EACH CLASS THAT I	RATING
1. Am following a plan.	
2. Present and explain the information simply and carefully.	
3. Use examples to help you understand the information presented.	
4. Use a step-by-step procedure throughout the lesson.	
5. Encourage you to ask questions when you do not understand.	
6. Stay with a concept until you understand.	
7. Repeat terms, provide several examples, and use visuals to help you understand the information.	
8. Stop often to review information before moving to a new topic.	
9. Ask questions to determine if you or other students understand.	
10. Stress the important points to remember.	

Name: _____

School: _____

Directions: Check the set of descriptors which best describes you as a middle school teacher. As a middle school teacher, I . . . .

Performance Area	Levels of Performance			
	Weak	Satisfactory	Strong	Excellent
A. Demonstrate mastery of subject matter.	a. Have a limited understanding of content area.	a. Have an adequate understanding of content area. b. Have a limited grasp of the structure of the discipline. c. Have achieved limited mastery of basic competencies. d. Rely on a few methods to teach content. e. Utilize one textbook and perhaps another resource.	a. Understand content area. b. Understand structure of curriculum area. c. Appropriately apply knowledge from curriculum area. d. Have knowledge and mastery of many basic competencies in curriculum area. e. Select methods which reinforce student understanding.	a. Understand structure of content area. b. Have mastered all basic competencies in curriculum area. c. Analyze curriculum area to more effectively match content to individual developmental needs. d. Consistently and successfully communicate knowledge and information on curriculum area. e. Select a wide variety of methods which enhance each student's understanding. f. Show persistence in obtaining Information and knowledge from various sources.
B. Work effectively as a team member.	a. Am cooperative only in situations which benefit self. b. Seem unaware of other teachers' needs. c. Seem unaware of activities being conducted by other teachers. d. Appear disinterested in helping colleagues.	a. Am aware of colleagues and communicate with few. b. Assist when asked. c. Share when asked a question. d. Accomplish own activities without regard for what other teachers are doing. e. Am concerned with own activities.	a. Am cooperative. b. Share ideas and materials. c. Attend planning sessions. d. Volunteer to assist. e. Am flexible. f. Appear interested In colleagues.	a. Consistently cooperate with each team member. b. Willingly share ideas and materials. c. Participate in planning sessions. d. Willingly share responsibility (lunch duty, recess, etc.). e. Perceive needs of team members and respond. f. Am flexible and adapt to change in schedules. g. Show a concern for colleagues.
C. Accept and Implement suggestions for self-improvement.	a. Listen to recommendations/suggestions after several feedback conferences. b. Avoid constructive criticism. c. Have difficulty analyzing own behavior in the classroom; prefer not to engage in such activities. d. Rarely alter teaching behavior, interactions, etc., even after extensive conferencing.	a. Rarely ask for recommendations/suggestions. b. Discuss strengths and weaknesses when prompted. c. Have difficulty in accepting constructive criticism. d. Implement few suggestions offered.	a. Ask for recommendations/suggestions. b. Am willing to discuss strengths and weaknesses. c. Implement many suggestions. d. Am aware of learning outcomes. e. Review effectiveness of daily and unit plan. f. Accept constructive criticism.	a. Regularly ask for recommendations/suggestions about interaction with peers, students, parents. b. Openly discuss strengths and weaknesses in instructional activities. c. Alter teaching methods/styles based on feedback. d. Diagnose individual learning outcomes. e. Initiate self-analysis of daily and unit plans. f. Accept and even encourage constructive criticism. g. Analyze the relationship between achievement gains and instructional effectiveness.

52

D. Demonstrate a sincere interest in teaching.	a. Ignore opportunities to reinforce student behavior. b. Teach to large group, neglecting individual needs. c. Make decisions inconsistently. d. Attend meetings, but not regularly. e. Ignore reference materials and professional journals.	a. Offer limited reinforcement to students. b. Am aware of student needs. c. Complete assignments with prompting. d. Make decisions, but reluctantly. e. Attend meetings. f. Have a limited interest in professional journals.	a. Am enthusiastic about students and schooling. b. Reinforce student behavior. c. Am aware of student needs and try to meet them. d. Attend meetings and participate. e. Prepare assignments in advance. f. Am aware, and understand program goals. g. Make decisions. h. Occasionally ask questions. i. Peruse journals and show an interest.	a. Demonstrate positive attitudes toward students and schooling. b. Am enthusiastic about teaching and being with students. c. Consistently reinforce student behavior. d. Recognize and try to meet individual student needs. e. Have assignments prepared well in advance of due date. f. Initiate questions to maintain team discussions. g. Seek suggestions, ideas, and information. h. Share ideas, materials, and suggestions. i. Understand and implement program goals. j. Make efficient, rapid decisions. k. Am a positive model. l. Keep current and read professional journals. m. Willingly attend meetings and enthusiastically participate.
E. Perform assigned tasks with promptness and responsibility.	a. Often am late for classes and activities. b. Often am late for meetings and conferences. c. Often miss due date for assignments and other tasks. d. Have difficulty in keeping records (often do not even keep records). e. Ignore school policies. f. Seem unaware of other teachers' needs.	a. Often arrive just in time for classes and activities but may be occasionally late. b. Often arrive on time for meetings and conferences. c. Complete assignments with prompting. d. Keep records with prompting. e. Need to be reminded about school policies. f. Assist when asked. g. Am concerned with own activities.	a. Arrive before classes and activities begin. b. Arrive before meetings and conferences begin. c. Prepare assignment in advance. d. Am dependable. e. Know school policies. f. Keep records up-to-date. g. Appear interested in colleagues.	a. Consistently arrive before classes and activities begin. b. Consistently arrive before meetings and conferences begin. c. Am consistently dependable in carrying out tasks. d. Have assignments prepared well in advance of due date. e. Adhere to school policies. f. Prepare and keep accurate records. g. Willingly share responsibility. h. Perceive needs of team members and respond.

TEACHER SKILLS CHECKLIST

Directions: After reading each item, check the most appropriate column.

Needs improvement	Strong	Outstanding	
			1. Planning
			2. Physical communication
			A. Eye contact
			B. Facial expression
			C. Purposeful movement
			D. Identify distracting mannerisms
			3. Vocal communication
			A. Vocal variety (expressiveness—monotony)
			B. Distracting vocal behavior (uh, sing-song, OK, etc.)
			4. Verbal communication
			A. Grammar and usage
			B. Pronunciation
			5. Responsiveness
			A. Listening to students
			B. Feedback responses
			6. Adaptiveness
			General ability to adjust, modify communication in terms of students' responses, tact.
			7. Teaching techniques
			A. Motivation
			B. Giving directions
			C. Questioning skills
			D. Use of materials
			E. Student participation
			8. Classroom management
			A. Locating the source of discipline problems
			B. Dealing with discipline problems
			C. Physical arrangement of room

SELF-ASSESSMENT INSTRUMENT:
DIAGNOSING THE LESSON

Name: _____ Date: _____

Lesson Topic: _____ Class Size: _____

Use the following scale to rate the lesson:

5 = Superior   4 = Good   3 = Average   2 = Below average   1 = Poor

Include written comments in the space provided. Use the back of the form if necessary. Be specific in comments and give examples if possible. Offer suggestions for improving the lesson.

	Rating	Comments
1. Was I enthusiastic in presenting the the material?		
2. Was the method of introducing the lesson interesting in itself?		
3. Did I present the topic in a manner that promoted student understanding?		
4. Was the introduction connected with the body of the lesson?		
5. Was the introduction presented in a way that helps retain the material in the body of the lesson?		
6. Did I ask a large number of questions?		
7. Did I probe for higher-order responses?		
8. Did I use a variety of reinforcers?		
9. Did I wait for pupil responses?		
10. Did I use verbal reinforcement of student responses?		
11. Did I use nonverbal reinforcement (facial expression and gestures) of student responses?		

55

	Rating	Comments
12. Did I use refocusing techniques to emphasize a point, both verbal and nonverbal?		
13. Did I use a variety of techniques? Did I use several activities such as games, board work, role play?		
14. Did I use both oral and visual stimuli (words on chalkboard, objects, pictures)?		
15. Did I review the major points and ideas throughout the lesson?		
16. Did I allow students the opportunity to demonstrate what they have learned (providing for student summary or practice of new learning)?		
17. Did I summarize the class discussion including the major points covered by teacher and class?		

Specific suggestions for improvement:

2. OTHER TEACHER SELF-ASSESSMENT INSTRUMENTS

Philosophical Belief System

The Scale of Cognitive Structures is a questionnaire designed to identify an individual's philosophical orientation. Items are keyed to represent three dominant philosophical strains in American culture: traditionalism, pragmatism/progressivism, and existentialism. The instrument and manual may be obtained from

> Scale of Cognitive Structures
> O. P. Esteves
> College of Education
> Texas Tech University
> Lubbock, TX 79409

Interpersonal Awareness Traits

The Fundamental Interpersonal Relations Orientation-Behavior (FIRO-B) is designed to measure an individual's characteristic behavior toward others in the areas of inclusion, control, and affection. This instrument is also designed to stress relationships between people, such as compatability or coefficiency. It may be obtained from

> Fundamental Interpersonal Relations Orientation-Behavior (FIRO-B)
> William C. Schutz
> Consulting Psychological Press
> 577 College Avenue
> Palo Alto, CA 94306

Self-Concept

The Tennessee Self-Concept Scale is self-scoring and is composed of 100 self-descriptive statements, which the teacher uses to portray a picture of him/herself. The scale provides a profile which shows comparative data concerning physical self, moral-ethical self, personal self, family self, social self, identity—what he or she is, self-satisfaction—how he or she accepts him/herself, and behavior—how he or she acts. The instrument may be obtained from

> Tennessee Self-Concept Scale
> William H. Fritts
> Counselor Recordings and Tests
> Box 6184, Acklen Station
> Nashville, TN 37212

Learning Style

The Productivity Environmental Preference Survey (PEPS) assesses the individual adult's personal preferences for each of 21 different elements in four major areas. This survey identifies how adults prefer to function, learn, concentrate, and perform in their occupational or educational activities in the following areas: immediate environment (sound, temperature, light, and design); emotionality (motivation, responsibility, persistence, and need for either structure or flexibility); sociological needs (self-oriented, colleague-oriented, authority-oriented, and/or combined ways); and physical needs (perceptual preference(s), time of day, intake, and mobility). The instrument may be obtained from

> Productivity Environmental Preference Survey
> Gary Price, Rita Dunn, and Kenneth Dunn
> Price Systems, Inc.
> Box 3067
> Lawrence, KS 66044

Another instrument for diagnosing learning style is the Learning Style Inventory (LSI), a nine-item self-description questionnaire. Each item asks respondents to order four words in a way that best describes his or her learning style. The LSI measures an individual's relative emphasis on four learning abilities: concrete experience (CE), reflective observation (RO), abstract conceptualization (AC), and active experimentation (AE), plus two combination scores that indicate the extent to which an individual emphasizes abstractness over concreteness (AC-CE) and action over reflection (AE-RO). The instrument may be obtained from

> Learning Style Inventory
> David A. Kolb
> McBer and Company
> 137 Newbury Street
> Boston, MA 02116

Teaching Style

The Teaching Style Inventory (TSI) provides a profile with nine major elements comprising an individual's teaching style. These elements are instructional planning, teaching methods, student groupings, room design, teaching environment, evaluation techniques, educational philosophy, teaching characteristics, and student preference. The instrument may be obtained from

> Teaching Style Inventory
> Rita and Kenneth Dunn
> Learning Styles Network
> School of Education and Human Services
> St. John's University
> Jamaica, NY 11439

Psychological Constructs

The Tuckman Teacher Feedback Form (TTFF) describes the teacher as a structurer, the teacher as a problemsolver, and four ways that teachers can deal with problems of control, interpersonal relations, and ambiguity. This instrument is composed of 28 paired adjectives, each pair representing a personal construct that can be used to construe the teacher's behavior. It may be obtained from

Tuckman Teacher Feedback Form
Bruce W. Tuckman
School of Education
Bernard Baruch College—CUNY
17 Lexington Avenue
New York, NY 10010

BIBLIOGRAPHY

1. Alexander, W. M., and George, P. S. *The Exemplary Middle School*. New York: Holt, Rinehart and Winston, 1981.
2. Allen, Dwight, and Ryan, Kevin. *Microteaching*. Reading, Mass.: Addison-Wesley, 1969.
3. Amidon, Edmund, and Flanders, Ned A. *The Role of the Teacher in the Classroom*. Minneapolis: Paul S. Amidon and Associates, 1963.
4. Arlin, Marshall. "Teacher Transition Can Disrupt Time Flow in Classrooms." *American Educational Research Journal* 16, no. 1 (Winter 1979): 42–56.
5. Askins, Billy E. "Teacher Self-Assessment Data: Bases for Designing a Personal Long-Range Professional Development Program." Paper presented at annual meeting of American Association of Colleges for Teacher Education, 1983.
6. Bailey, Gerald D. *Teacher Self-Assessment: A Means for Improving Classroom Instruction*. Washington, D.C.: National Education Association, 1981.
7. _____. *Teacher-Designed Student Feedback: A Strategy for Improving Classroom Instruction*. Washington, D.C.: National Education Association, 1983.
8. Barr, R., and Dreeben, R. "Instruction in Classrooms." In *Review of Research in Education*, edited by L. Shulman. vol. 5. Itasca, Ill.: Peacock, 1977.
9. Beach, Don, and Reinhartz, Judy. "Improving Instructional Effectiveness: A Self-Assessment Procedure." *Illinois School Research and Development Journal* 19, no. 1 (Fall 1982): 5–12.
10. Beck, C. M.; Crittenden, B. S.; and Sullivan, E. V., eds. *Moral Education: Interdisciplinary Approaches*. New York: Newman Press, 1971.
11. Blue, Terry W. *The Teaching and Learning Process*. Washington, D.C.: National Education Association, 1981.
12. Brooks, Martin; Fusco, Ester; and Grennon, Jacqueline. "Cognitive Levels Matching." *Educational Leadership* 40, no. 8 (May 1983): 5.
13. Brophy, Jere E. *Advances in Teacher Effectiveness Research*. Occasional Paper No. 18. East Lansing, Mich.: College of Education, Michigan State University, 1979.
13a. _____. "Teacher Behavior and Student Learning." *Educational Leadership* 37, no. 1 (October 1979): 33–38.
14. Bruner, Jerome. *The Process of Education*. Cambridge, Mass.: Harvard University Press, 1960.
15. _____. *Beyond the Information Given: Studies in Psychology of Knowing*. New York: W. W. Norton, 1973.
16. Burkhard, M. I. "Discernment of Teacher Characteristics by T.A.T. Sequence Analysis." *Journal of Educational Psychology* 53 (December 1962): 279–87.
17. Caldwell, Janet H.; Huitt, W. G.; and Graeber, Anna O. "Time Spent in Learning: Implications from Research." *Elementary School Journal* 82, no. 5 (1982): 471–79.

18. Cogan, Morris. *Clinical Supervision.* Boston: Houghton Miffln, 1973.
19. Cruickshank, Donald, et al. *Reflective Teaching.* Bloomington, Ind.: Phi Delta Kappa, 1981.
20. Davis, Robert H.; Alexander, Lawrence, T.; and Yelon, Stephen L. *Learning System Design: An Approach to the Improvement of Instruction.* New York: McGraw-Hill, 1974.
21. Dembo, Myron H. *Teaching for Learning: Applying Educational Psychology in the Classroom.* Santa Monica, Calif.: Goodyear Publishing Co., 1981.
22. Duckett, Willard R. *Observation and the Evaluation of Teaching.* Bloomington, Ind.: Phi Delta Kappa, 1980.
23. Eisner, Elliot. "The Art and Craft of Teaching." *Educational Leadership* 40, no. 4 (January 1983): 4–14.
24. Epstein, H. T. "Phrenoblysis: Special Brain and Mind Growth Periods: Human Brain and Skull Development." *Developmental Psychology* 7 (1974): 207–16.
25. _____. "Growth Spurts During Brain Development: Implications for Educational Policy and Practice." In *Education and the Brain,* edited by J. Chall. 79th Yearbook, Part II. National Society for the Study of Education. Chicago: University of Chicago Press, 1978.
26. Erickson, Erik. *Childhood and Society.* New York: Norton, 1950.
27. _____. *Identity: Youth and Crisis.* New York, Norton, 1968.
28. Evertson, C., and Anderson, L. *The Classroom Organization Study: Interim Progress Report.* Report N. 6002. Austin: Research and Development Center for Teacher Education, University of Texas at Austin, 1978.
29. Forisha-Kovach, Barbara. *The Experience of Adolescence.* Dallas, Texas: Scott, Foresman and Co., 1983.
30. Gage, Nathaniel. *The Scientific Basis for the Art of Teaching.* New York: Teachers College Press, 1977.
30a. Gall, Meredith D.; Dunning, Barbara; and Weathersby, Rita. *Higher Cognitive Questioning, Teacher's Handbook.* Beverly Hills, Calif.: Macmillan Educational Services (for Far West Regional Laboratory), 1971.
31. Harris, Ben, and Hill, Jane. *Developmental Teacher Evaluation Kit (DeTEK).* Austin: Southwest Educational Development Laboratory, 1983.
32. Heath, Philip A., and Weible, Thomas. *Developing Social Responsibility in the Middle School: A Unit Teaching Approach.* Rev. ed. Washington, D.C.: National Education Association, 1983.
33. Henak, Richard M. *Lesson Planning for Meaningful Variety in Teaching.* Washington, D.C.: National Education Association, 1980.
34. Hosford, Phillip. "The Silent Curriculum: Its Impact on Teaching the Basics." *Educational Leadership* (December 1978): 213.
35. Jenkins, Gladys Gardner; Schacter, Helen S.; and Bauer, William W. *These Are Your Children.* Glenview, Ill.: Scott, Foresman and Co., 1966.
36. Joyce, Bruce, and Showers, Beverly. "The Coaching of Teaching." *Educational Leadership* 40, no. 1 (October 1982): 4–10.
37. _____, and _____. "Improving Inservice Training: The Messages of Research." *Educational Leadership* (February 1980): 379–84.
38. _____, and Weil, Marsha. *Models of Teaching.* Englewood Cliffs, N.J.: Prentice-Hall, 1980.

39. Kennedy, J. J., et al. "Additional Investigations into the Nature of Teacher Clarity." *Journal of Educational Research* 72 (September/October 1978): 3–10.
40. Kepner, Henry S., Jr., ed. *Computers in the Classroom.* Washington, D.C.: National Education Association, 1982.
41. Kohlberg, Lawrence. "Development of Moral Character and Moral Ideology." In *Review of Child Development Research,* edited by M. L. Hoffman and L. W. Hoffman. New York: Russell Sage Foundation, 1964.
42. Kohut, Sylvester, Jr. *The Middle School: A Bridge Between Elementary and Secondary Schools.* Washington, D.C.: National Education Association, 1976.
43. Kounin, J. *Discipline and Group Management in Classrooms.* New York: Holt, Rinehart and Winston, 1970.
44. Lockwood, A. "The Effects of Values Clarification and Moral Development Curricula on School-Age Subjects: A Critical Review of Recent Research." *Review of Educational Research* 48 (1978): 325–64.
45. McConnell, J. "Relationships Between Selected Teacher Behaviors and Attitudes/Achievements of Algebra Classes." Paper presented at annual meeting of American Educational Research Association, 1977.
46. McEwin, C. Kenneth, and Alexander, William M. *The Status of Middle/Junior High School Teacher Education Programs: A Research Report.* Boone, N.C.: Appalachian State University, 1982.
47. Manatt, Richard P. *Evaluating Teacher Performance.* Washington, D.C.: Association for Supervision and Curriculum Development, 1981. Videotape.
48. _____. "Manatt's Exercise in Selecting Teacher Performance Evaluation Criteria Based on Effective Teaching Research." Albuquerque, N.M.: National Symposium for Professionals in Evaluation and Research, November 1981.
49. Martorella, Peter H. "Teaching Concepts." In *Classroom Teaching Skills: A Handbook,* edited by James M. Cooper. Lexington, Mass.: D.C. Heath and Co., 1977.
50. Medley, Donald, and Mitzel, H. E. "Techniques for Measuring Classroom Behavior." *Journal of Educational Psychology* 49 (April 1965): 86–92.
51. _____. *Teacher Competence and Teacher Effectiveness: A Process-Product Research.* Washington, D.C.: American Association of Colleges for Teacher Education, 1977.
52. _____. *Teacher Competency Testing the Teacher Educators.* Charlottesville, Va.: Educational Research, School of Education, University of Virginia, 1982.
53. Reynolds, John. "In Search of Mr. (Ms.) Goodteacher." *Action in Teacher Education* 2, no. 1 (Winter 1979–1980): 35–38.
54. Rosenshine, Barak. "Enthusiastic Teaching: A Research Review." *School Review* (August 1970): 499–514.
55. _____, and Furst, Norma. "Research in Teacher Performance Criteria." In *Research in Teacher Education,* edited by B. O. Smith. Englewood Cliffs, N.J.: Prentice-Hall, 1971.
56. Rouk, Ullik. "Separate Studies Show Similar Results of Teacher Effectiveness." *Educational R & D Report* 2, no. 2 (Spring 1979): 6–10.
57. Rowe, Mary Budd. "Wait Time and Rewards as Instructional Variables, Their Influence on Language, Logic and Fate Control: Part One—Wait Time." *Journal of Research in Science Teaching* 11 (1974): 81–94.

58. Rubin, Louis. "Artistry in Teaching." *Educational Leadership* 40, no. 4 (January 1983): 44–51.
59. Ryans, David G. *Characteristics of Teachers*. Washington, D.C.: American Council on Education, 1960.
60. Sale, Larry L. *Introduction to Middle School Teaching*. Columbus, Ohio: Charles Merrill, 1979.
61. Silvernail, David L. *Teaching Styles as Related to Student Achievement*. Washington, D.C.: National Education Association, 1979.
62. Soar, Robert, and Soar, Ruth. *Classroom Behavior, Pupil Characteristics, and Pupil Growth for the School Year and for the Summer*. University of Florida, 1973. In *JSAS Catalog of Selected Documents in Psychology*, vol. 5, 1975; 200-MS.
63. Stallings, J. "Teaching Basic Reading Skills in the Secondary Schools." Paper presented at annual meeting of American Educational Research Association, 1978.
64. Toepfer, Conrad F., Jr. "Brain Growth Periodization Data: Some Suggestions for Reorganizing Middle Grades Education." *High School Journal* 63 (March 1980): 224–26.
65. Valentine, J.; Clark, D. C.; Nickerson, N.; and Keefe, J. W. *The Middle Level Principalship: A Survey of Principals and Programs*. Reston, Va.: National Association of Secondary School Principals, 1981.
66. Walberg, Herbert J.; Schiller, Diane; and Haertzel, Geneva D. "The Quiet Revolution in Educational Research." *Phi Delta Kappan* 61 (November 1979): 179–83.
67. Wilen, William W. *Questioning Skills, for Teachers*. Washington, D.C.: National Education Association, 1982.

nea PROFESSIONAL LIBRARY
Stock No. 1688-2-00